DRESS |
EL VESTIRSE

Grow a bilingual vocabulary by:

- **Looking** at pictures and words
- **Talking** about what you see
- **Touching** and naming objects
- **Using** questions to extend learning...
  Ask questions that invite children
  to share information.
  Begin your questions with words like...
  who, what, when, where and how.

Aumenta tu vocabulario bilingüe:

- **Mirando** las imágenes y las palabras
- **Hablando** de lo que ves
- **Tocando** y nombrando los objetos
- **Usando** preguntas para aumentar el aprendizaje...
  Usa preguntas que inviten a los niños a compartir
  la información.
  Empieza tus frases con el uso de estas palabras:
  ¿quién? ¿qué? ¿cuándo? ¿dónde? y ¿cómo?

These books support a series of educational games by Learning Props.
Estos libros refuerzan una serie de juegos educativos desarrollados por Learning Props.
Learning Props, L.L.C., P.O. Box 774, Racine, WI 53401-0774
1-877-776-7750   www.learningprops.com

Created by/Creado por: Bev Schumacher, Learning Props, L.L.C.
Graphic Design/Diseñadora gráfica: Bev Kirk
Images/Fotos: Bev Kirk, Jane Lund, Hemera Technologies Inc., Photos.com
Spanish Translation/Traducción al español: Myriam Sosa, Rosana Sartirana

Library of Congress Control Number 2008907374   ISBN 978-1-935292-05-0

LEARNING ★PROPS★

Babies wear...
Los bebés usan...

onesie
el mameluco/
el enterito

sleeper
el pijama/
el enterito

sweater
el suéter

booties
los escarpines

bib
el babero

snowsuit
el traje para
la nieve

diaper
el pañal

shoes
los zapatos

 # On my hands I wear...
En las manos me pongo...

mittens
los mitones/los guantes

rings
los anillos

gloves
los guantes

watch
el reloj

bracelet
la pulsera

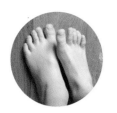

On my feet I wear...
En los pies me pongo...

sandals
las sandalias

cowboy boots
las botas vaqueras

slippers
las pantuflas/
las chinelas

flip flops
las chanclas/
las ojotas

snow boots
las botas
para la nieve

shoes
los zapatos

in-line skates
los patines en línea

soccer shoes
los botines de fútbol/
los zapatos de fútbol

roller skates
los patines

socks
los calcetines

ballet slippers
los zapatos
de ballet

hockey skates
los patines de hockey

ice skates
los patines para
el hielo

figure skates
los patines para
el hielo

On my head I wear...
En la cabeza me pongo...

knitted hat
el gorro tejido

hat
el sombrero

sun visor
la visera

glasses
los lentes/los anteojos

bike helmet
el casco
para bicicleta

sunglasses
los lentes de sol/
las gafas oscuras

baseball cap
la gorra
de béisbol

goggles
las gafas
para nadar

headband
la diadema/
la vincha

cowboy hat
el sombrero
vaquero

sun hat
la gorra para
el sol

earmuffs
las orejeras

mask
la máscara

# On my top I wear...
En la parte de arriba me pongo...

short sleeved shirt
la camiseta playera

long sleeved shirt
la camisa de
manga larga

sleeveless shirt
la camiseta
sin mangas

hooded jacket
la chamarra con capucha/
la campera

buttoned up shirt
la camisa de botones

sweatshirt
el buzo/
la sudadera

T-shirt
la camiseta

sweater
el suéter/
el jersey

vest
el chaleco

backpack
la mochila

 # On my bottom I wear...
En la parte de abajo me pongo...

skirt
la falda/la pollera

belt
el cinturón/el cinto

pants
los pantalones

shorts
los pantalones cortos/
los shorts

underwear
los calzones

boxers
los calzoncillos

sweatpants
los pantalones de ejercicios/los pants

jeans
los pantalones de mezclilla

When it is warm I wear...
Cuando hace calor me pongo...

sundress
la solera/
el vestido

tank top
la camiseta
sin mangas

swimsuit
el traje de baño

shorts
los pantalones cortos/
los shorts

flip flops
las chanclas/las ojotas

When it rains I use...
Cuando llueve uso...

umbrella
el paraguas

raincoat
el impermeable

rain boots
las botas de lluvia

When it is cold I wear...
Cuando hace frío me pongo...

hat
el gorro/
la gorra

earmuffs
las orejeras

snow pants
los pantalones
para la nieve

coat
la chaqueta/el abrigo

scarf
la bufanda

snow boots
las botas para
la nieve

mittens
los mitones/
los guantes

gloves
los guantes

At night I wear...
En la noche me pongo...

nightgown
el camisón/
la bata de dormir

pajamas
los pijamas/los piyamas

robe
la bata de baño

slippers
las pantuflas/
las chinelas

When I play I wear...
Cuando juego me pongo...

paint smock
el delantal para pintar/
el blusón para pintar

boa
la boa de plumas/
el boa de plumas

lei
el collar
de flores

sportswear
el equipo
deportivo

dance clothes
el traje de baile

firefighter
helmet
el casco de
bombero

life jacket
el chaleco
salvavidas

Girls could wear...
Las niñas pueden usar...

slip
la enagua/
el fondo

headband
la diadema/
la vincha

jewelry
las joyas/
las alhajas

dress
el vestido

blouse
la blusa

jumper
el jumper

skirt
la falda/
la pollera

bow
el moño

tights
las pantimedias/
las medias largas

shoes
los zapatos

purse
la bolsa/
la cartera

Boys could wear...
Los niños pueden usar...

shirt
la camisa

sweater
el suéter/
el jersey

ties
las corbatas

overalls
el overol/
el mameluco

suspenders
los tirantes/
los tiradores

shoes
los zapatos

suit
el traje

pronunciation la pronunciación

Dress Up/**Dress Uhp** *El Vestirse*/Ayl Vays-**teer**-say

babies wear/**bay**-bees **wair** los bebés usan/lohs bay-**bays** oo-sahn

on my hands I wear/**on mye hands eye wair** en las manos me pongo/ayn lahs **mah**-nohs may **pohn**-goh

on my feet I wear/**on mye feet eye wair** en los pies me pongo/ayn lohs pee-**ays** may **pohn**-goh

on my head I wear/**on mye hed eye wair** en la cabeza me pongo/ayn lahs kah-**bay**-sah may **pohn**-goh

on my top I wear/**on mye top eye wair** en la parte de arriba me pongo/ayn lah **pahr**-tay day ah-**rree**-bah may **pohn**-goh

on my bottom I wear/**on mye bot**-uhm **eye wair** en la parte de abajo me pongo/ayn lah **pahr**-tay day ah-**bah**-hoh may **pohn**-goh

when it is warm I wear/**wen it iz worm eye wair** cuando hace calor me pongo/koo-**ahn**-doh ah-**say** kah-**lohr** may **pohn**-goh

when it rains I use/**wen it raynz eye yus** cuando llueve uso/koo-**ahn**-doh yoo-**ay**-vay oo-soh

when it is cold I wear/**wen it iz kohld eye wair** cuando hace frío me pongo/koo-**ahn**-doh ah-**say free**-oh may **pohn**-goh

at night I wear/**at nite eye wair** en la noche me pongo/ayn lah **noh**-shay may **pohn**-goh

when I play I wear/**wen eye play eye wair** cuando juego me pongo/koo-**ahn**-doh hoo-**ay**-goh may **pohn**-goh

girls could wear/**gurls kud wair** las niñas pueden usar/lahs **nee**-nyahs poo-**ay**-dayn oo-**sahr**

boys could wear/**bois kud wair** los niños pueden usar/lohs **nee**-nyohs poo-**ay**-dayn oo-**sahr**

match their clothes/**mach THair klohz** encuentra lo que ellos estan usando/ayn-koo-**ayn**-trah loh kay **ay**-yohs ays-**tahn** oo-**sahn**-doh

---

backpack/**bak**-pak la mochila/lah moh-**shee**-lah

ballet slippers/**bal**-lay **slip**-urz los zapatos de ballet/lohs sah-**pah**-tohs day bah-**layt**

baseball cap/**bayss**-bawl **kap** la gorra de béisbol/lah **goh**-rrah day **bays**-bohl

belt/**belt** el cinturón, el cinto/ayl seen-too-**rohn**, ayl **seen**-toh

bib/**bib** el babero/ayl bah-**bay**-roh

bike helmet/**bike hel**-mit el casco para bicicleta/ayl **kahs**-koh **pah**-rah bee-see-**klay**-tah

blouse/**blouss** la blusa/lah **bloo**-sah

boa/**boh**-uh la boa de plumas, el boa de plumas/lah **boh**-ah day **ploo**-mahs, ayl **boh**-ah day **ploo**-mahs

booties/**boot**-eez los escarpines/lohs ays-kahr-**pee**-nays

bow/**boh** el moño/ayl **moh**-nyoh

boxers/**boks**-urz los calzoncillos/lohs kahl-sohn-**see**-yohs

bracelet/**brayss**-lit la pulsera/lah pool-**say**-rah

buttoned up shirt/**buht**-uhnd **uhp shurt** la camisa de botones/lah kah-**mee**-sah day boh-**toh**-nays

coat/**koht** la chaqueta, el abrigo/lah shah-**kay**-tah, ayl ah-**bree**-goh

cowboy boots/**kou**-boi **bootz** las botas vaqueras/lahs **boh**-tahs vah-**kay**-rahs

cowboy hat/**kou**-boi **hat** el sombrero vaquero/ayl sohm-**bray**-roh vah-**kay**-roh

dance clothes/**danss klohz** el traje de baile/ayl **trah**-hay day **bah**-ee-lay

diaper/**dye**-pur el pañal/ayl pah-**nyahl**

dress/**dress** el vestido/ayl vays-**tee**-doh

earmuffs/**ihr**-muhfss las orejeras/lahs oh-ray-**hay**-rahs

figure skates/**fig**-yur **skaytss** los patines para el hielo/lohs pah-**tee**-nays **pah**-rah ayl ee-**ay**-loh

firefighter helmet/**fire**-fite-ur **hel**-mit el casco de bombero/ayl **kahs**-koh day bohm-**bay**-roh

flip flops/**flip flops** las chanclas, las ojotas/lahs **shahn**-klahs, lahs oh-**hoh**-tahs

glasses/**glass**-iz los lentes, los anteojos/lohs **layn**-tays, lohs ahn-tay-**oh**-hohs

gloves/**gluhvz** los guantes/lohs goo-**ahn**-tays

goggles/**gog**-uhlz las gafas para nadar/lahs **gah**-fahs **pah**-rah nah-**dahr**

hat/**hat** el sombrero/ayl sohm-**bray**-roh
el gorro, la gorra/ayl **goh**-rroh, lah **goh**-rrah

headband/**hed**-band la diadema, la vincha/lah dee-ah-**day**-mah, lah **veen**-shah

hockey skates/**hok**-ee **skaytss** los patines de hockey/lohs pah-**tee**-nays day **hoh**-kee

hooded jacket/**hud**-ed **jak**-it la chamarra con capucha, la campera/lah shah-**mah**-rrah kohn kah-**poo**-shah, lah kahm-**pay**-rah

ice skates/**eyess skaytss** los patines para el hielo/
lohs pah-**tee**-nays **pah**-rah ayl ee-**ay**-loh

in-line skates/**in**-line **skaytss** los patines en línea/
lohs pah-**tee**-nays ayn **lee**-nay-ah

jeans/**jeenz** los pantalones de mezclilla/
lohs pahn-tah-**loh**-nays day mays-**klee**-yah

jewelry/**joo**-uhl-ree las joyas, las alhajas/lahs **hoh**-yahs,
lahs ah-**lah**-has

jumper/**juhm**-pur el jumper/ayl **yahm**-payr

knitted hat/**nit**-id **hat** el gorro tejido/ayl **goh**-rroh
tay-**hee**-doh

lei/**lay** el collar de flores/ayl koh-**yahr** day **floh**-rays

life jacket/**life jak**-it el chaleco salvavidas/
ayl shah-**lay**-koh sahl-vah-**vee**-dahs

long sleeved shirt/**lawng sleevd shurt** la camisa de
manga larga/lah kah-**mee**-sah day **mahn**-gah **lahr**-gah

mask/**mask** la máscara/lah **mahs**-kah-rah

mittens/**mit**-uhnz los mitones, los guantes/
lohs mee-**toh**-nays, lohs goo-**ahn**-tays

nightgown/**nite**-goun el camisón, la bata de dormir/
ayl kah-mee-**sohn**, lah **bah**-tah day dohr-**meer**

onesie/**wuhn**-ze el mameluco, el enterito/
ayl mah-may-**loo**-koh, ayl ayn-tay-**ree**-toh

overalls/**oh**-vur-awlz el overol, el mameluco/
ayl oh-vay-**rohl**, ayl mah-may-**loo**-koh

paint smock/**paynt smok** el delantal para pintar,
el blusón para pintar/ayl day-lahn-**tahl pah**-rah
peen-**tahr**, ayl bloo-**sohn pah**-rah peen-**tahr**

pajamas/puh-**jam**-uhz los pijamas, los piyamas/
lohs pee-**hah**-mahs, lohs pee-**yah**-mahs

pants/**pants** los pantalones/lohs pahn-tah-**loh**-nays

purse/**purss** la bolsa, la cartera/lah **bohl**-sah,
lah kahr-**tay**-rah

rain boots/**rayn bootz** las botas de lluvia/
lahs **boh**-tahs day **yoo**-vee-ah

raincoat/**rayn**-koht el impermeable/
ayl eem-payr-may-**ah**-blay

rings/**ringz** los anillos/lohs ah-**nee**-yohs

robe/**robe** la bata de baño/lah **bah**-tah day **bah**-nyoh

roller skates/**roh**-lur **skaytss** los patines/
lohs pah-**tee**-nays

sandals/**san**-duhlz las sandalias/lahs sahn-**dah**-lee-ahs

scarf/**skarf** la bufanda/lah boo-**fahn**-dah

shirt/**shurt** la camisa/lah kah-**mee**-sah

shoes/**shooz** los zapatos/lohs sah-**pah**-tohs

short sleeved shirt/**short sleevd shurt** la camiseta
playera/lah kah-mee-**say**-tah plah-**yay**-rah

shorts/**shorts** los pantalones cortos, los shorts/
lohs pahn-tah-**loh**-nays **kohr**-tohs, lohs shohrts

skirt/**skurt** la falda, la pollera/lah **fahl**-dah,
lah poh-**yay**-rah

sleeper/**sleep**-ur el pijama, el enterito/ayl pee-**hah**-mah,
ayl ayn-tay-**ree**-toh

sleeveless shirt/**sleev**-liss **shurt** la camiseta sin mangas/
lah kah-mee-**say**-tah seen **mahn**-gahs

slip/**slip** la enagua, el fondo/lah ay-**nah**-goo-ah,
ayl **fohn**-doh

slippers/**slip**-urz las pantuflas, las chinelas/
lahs pahn-**too**-flahs, lahs shee-**nay**-lahs

snow boots/**snoh bootz** las botas para la nieve/
lahs **boh**-tahs **pah**-rah lah nee-**ay**-vay

snow pants/**snoh pants** los pantalones para la nieve/
lohs pahn-tah-**loh**-nays **pah**-rah lah nee-**ay**-vay

snowsuit/**snoh**-soot el traje para la nieve/ayl **trah**-hay
pah-rah lah nee-**ay**-vay

soccer shoes/**sok**-ur **shooz** los botines de fútbol,
los zapatos de fútbol/lohs boh-**tee**-nays day **foot**-bohl,
lohs sah-**pah**-tohs day **foot**-bohl

socks/**sokz** los calcetines/lohs kahl-say-**tee**-nays

sportswear/**sports**-wair el equipo deportivo/
ayl ay-**kee**-poh day-pohr-**tee**-voh

suit/**soot** el traje/ayl **trah**-hay

sun hat/**suhn hat** la gorra para el sol/lah **goh**-rrah
pah-rah ayl sohl

sun visor/**suhn vye**-zur la visera/lah vee-**say**-rah

sundress/**suhn**-dress la solera, el vestido/
lah soh-**lay**-rah, ayl vays-**tee**-doh

sunglasses/**suhn**-glass-iz los lentes de sol, las gafas
oscuras/lohs **layn**-tays day sohl, lahs **gah**-fahs
ohs-**koo**-rahs

suspenders/suh-**spen**-durz los tirantes, los tiradores/
lohs tee-**rahn**-tays, lohs tee-rah-**doh**-rays

sweater/**swet**-ur el suéter, el jersey/ayl soo-**ay**-tayr,
ayl **hayr**-say

sweatpants/**swet**-pants los pantalones de ejercicios,
los pants/lohs pahn-tah-**loh**-nays day
ay-hayr-**see**-see-ohs, lohs pahnts

sweatshirt/**swet**-shurt el buzo, la sudadera/ayl **boo**-soh,
lah soo-dah-**day**-rah

swimsuit/**swim**-soot el traje de baño/ayl **trah**-hay day
bah-nyoh

tank top/**tangk top** la camiseta sin mangas/
lah kah-mee-**say**-tah seen **mahn**-gahs

ties/**tyez** las corbatas/lahs kohr-**bah**-tahs

tights/**titess** las pantimedias, las medias largas/lahs
pahn-tee-**may**-dee-ahs, lahs **may**-dee-ahs **lahr**-gahs

T-shirt/**tee**-shurt la camiseta/lah kah-mee-**say**-tah

umbrella/uhm-**brel**-uh el paraguas/ayl pah-**rah**-goo-ahs

underwear/**uhn**-dur-wair los calzones/
lohs kahl-**soh**-nays

vest/**vest** el chaleco/ayl shah-**lay**-koh

watch/**woch** el reloj/ayl rray-**lohgh**

match their clothes
encuentra lo que ellos estan usando